Dear Mama,

Selected poems written by Cherry Carl
for sharing with loved ones

Cover art: art4crafts.com

Dear Mama . . .

This is dedicated to the memory of my mother, the reason for this collection of poetry. Please read it in sequence to fully understand its message.

This was originally published in 1986 and given to many friends and family members. Being able to write poetry is not a talent. It is a gift that is meant to be shared. This is my gift to you. If you'd like to share a poem, please feel free to do so. The original was printed on lavender parchment with my artwork. I like to think of it in that form, and I think my mother did, too. She loved to share it with her friends and with anyone who would listen. You know how mothers love to crow. Thanks to all who gave me invaluable insight and inspiration and for sharing your own personal thoughts and memories about your mamas.

For Mama,

For every woman

who has ever experienced

the joy of motherhood . . .

And for every person

who has ever been blessed

by a mother's love.

Dear Mama . . .

Those two words say it all.

Dear Mama,

Do you remember how blessed you felt when you knew that you were going to have a baby . . . and the joy and wonder of being closer to another human being for nine months than ever before . . . or since?

Oh, sweet baby, you'll come our way .

On some lovely sunlit day.

Your roots will be planted in love's rich soil

As your parents laugh, love, and toil.

You'll be nourished with warmth and caring that's wise

And your branches and leaves will reach for the skies.

Grow little one, with your face to the sun,

For your precious life has just begun.

And then that fateful day arrived . . .

As the evening changed to early morn,
My firstborn child, my son, was born.
As the morning sun lit up the sky,
I heard his strong and healthy cry!
A cry that filled my heart with mirth,
And forever changed my role on earth.
My sacred duty, my place in the sun,
Is to love and to nurture my newborn son.

Life has never been the same since I heard a cry

I heard a baby girl's first cry,
As the starlight filled the evening sky;
A cry announcing a healthy birth,
As God was lending you to this earth,
A cry that filled each tiny lung
With a song of life as yet unsung,
A cry that formed a bond for three . . .
The father, mother, and newborn thee.

The early years . . . God made mothers to get us through those years, blessing them with the patience and wisdom to guide us . . . as we tried to do everything for ourselves before we knew how . . . and especially when we had finally mastered the word "no."

The Early Years

God made mothers to get us through
Those rough and tumble years . . .
To soothe our wounds, dispel our fears,
And wipe away our woeful tears.

He gave to all a patient hand
With a very special goal . . .
To guide each precious little soul,
And keep them pure and whole.

He formed a bond between mother and child,
A bond of untold worth . . .
That began to grow from the moment of birth,
To strengthen our lives on earth.

The strength of that bond was often tested. We were such rascals at that age; our small hands upset anything that wasn't nailed down, and we tried your patience at every turn. You'd find a quiet moment for yourself, only to be interrupted. We'd come rushing in, dirty-faced, full of life, and ready for a hug.

Today, I felt it . . . that sweet-tasting joy.
'Twas given to me by a wiggly young boy.
With trust in his heart, this so special child,
Gave me his gift, so gentle, yet wild.
Tears filled my eyes, and my heart felt a tug
As I cherished the joy . . .
Of a "just because" hug!

We didn't always live up to your expectations, even though we tried so hard. You loved us anyway.

She wants me to be especially good.

And sometimes I am . . .

but not when I should.

She wants me to grow to be healthy and strong,

But I can eat junk food all day long!

She wants me to learn to be friendly and sweet,

So, sometimes, I smile at the people I meet.

She wants me to be so clean and so tidy,

So I make up my bed . . .

Every Tuesday and Friday!

She wants my respect and says to be kind,

But it's not always easy to keep that in mind.

This person is special . . . she's not like another.

She always loves me . . .

She's my friend and my mother!

Summer was a pleasant time of year for us. It often meant more work and little or no peace and quiet for you, but you encouraged us to experience those delicious days when . . .

School's Out!

You've worked and toiled this year at school
To master every task and tool . . .
Trying to give your every best
To every teacher, every test.
But have you found that lovely thing
That makes you want to laugh and sing,
To run and leap in joyous fun,
And feel the warmth of summer's sun?
This feeling comes when school days end,
And summer's just around the bend . . .
The ticklish joy of barefoot toes,
Ice cream cones, a sprinkler hose!
No more spelling or math for you,
Just lovely days to think and do.
Enjoy those days, but fill each one,
With caring and sharing in summer's sun.

There were times when you were caught up in the daily grind of household chores, forgetting what it was like to enjoy the small things. You'd hear the uninhibited laughter of your children, and for one carefree afternoon, you'd leave behind the dishes, the dust, and the dirty clothes. I cherish the memory of those afternoons when you'd take the time for a little regression therapy:

I join the joyful girls and boys,
And taste their timeless, endless joys,
Of colored eggs, games, and toys,
Puppy dogs, and children's noise.
Roller skates,
And lazy days
Of flying kites,
And wiggly ways.
My weary soul begins to sing . . .
When I take the time to play and swing.

Betwixt and between . . . that we were, so desperately wanting to be adults, yet hanging on to the joys of childhood . . . and there you were, not always understanding (who could?) but always there, ready to listen, to forgive, and to love.

Betwixt and Between

Oh, pretty girl, my lovely young teen,
You seem to be caught . . . betwixt and between.
For you've reached what they call the "in-between
stage,"
And where you fit is hard to gauge.
Oh, to be childish, with never a care
Of boyfriends and makeup and just what to wear,
Of quarrels with parents over trivial things,
And trying to handle what growing up brings.
We tell you to grow up but deny you the chance,
Especially when boys give you more than a glance.
We tell you to grow up and give you advice,
But can't tell you how to always feel nice.
"Fix that hair, wash your face, and please wear a
dress,"

Just doesn't fit in when your life seems a mess.

Betwixt or between, till you're one or the other,

Remember the friend you can find in your mother.

We clashed during those confusing teenage years and said things we shouldn't have . . . hurtful things we didn't really mean to say but couldn't take back, not even knowing . . .

Why . . .

Why do you say the things you do,

The things that hurt and tear in two?

When words are better left unsaid,

Your wrath and anger are left unfed.

They cannot grow unspoken, you see,

So please don't say those things to me!

I'm Not a Kid Anymore!

Birthdays for kids are often hairy,

With useless gifts from my Aunt Mary.

Grandmas and mother and brothers, too,

Don't always pick what's best for you.

I used to sigh and roll my eyes

At the things that were wrong in color and size.

I'd stuff them in closets,

And cram them in drawers

To be forever lost and seen no more.

But now I'm assertive in expressing my taste,

So gifts can never be bought in haste.

I'm old enough to pick and choose

What's right for me in color and hues.

There won't be gifts crammed in the drawer,

"Cause I'm sure not a little kid anymore!

There were other people in my life in those days, people who nourished and enriched my life. They opened the door of my mind, and I looked through the windows of the world. You couldn't understand why I needed to spend so much time with them, but you let me go, knowing that you couldn't hold on forever.

I Have a Someone

For every girl, there is a mother,

But, sometimes, when she needs another,

There's someone there with a helping hand

To hear her tales of life's demands.

She'll laugh with her and share the tears

That often flow in teenage years.

No matter what the young girl brings,

The secret woes, the joyful things,

This special someone cares for her

And lends her love, so strong and sure.

I have a someone of my own.

Because of her, I've changed and grown.

This someone means so much to me,

And makes me glad that I am me.

Thank you, Mama, for letting me have a someone.

Life could be upsetting, depressing, frustrating, and exhilarating, all in the same day. It was often more than we knew how to cope with calmly. Half the time, we didn't even know what was wrong.

You were always there . . .

Listening

I can see that you're carrying a burden of sadness today. I can see it in your walk, your face, and your eyes. They're crying out, "Help me with this problem. It's too big to handle alone." If I could, I'd pick it up and carry it for you so your troubled heart could rest . . . but I can't.

I can only listen and care, and perhaps, in your telling and my listening . . . the weight of your burden will diminish.

You taught us how to look at life, to see what choices we had and how to handle . . .

The Weight of it All

We all have troubles in our journeys through life,
But it's how we measure them
That determines their weight.

We can see them as boulders,
Crushing us with their size and dimension.

Or perhaps as small stones
To be considered lightly and tossed aside.

Better yet, as grains of sand,
To be ground into the soil of life,
Making it a smooth path to follow.

It was easier when the problems were as minor as a skinned knee or a broken toy, wasn't it? A warm hug or a soothing word was enough to solve the problems of the world of a five-year-old, but not anymore.

Yesterday's Child

Where is the one so wiggly and wild,
The one I knew as yesterday's child?
The one who curled up in my lap
For quiet time . . . to take a nap,
To talk of things and wonder why,
To build some dreams, to laugh and cry.

That squirmy one, so slender and small,
Has really grown to be quite tall.
No time to talk and wonder why . . .
She'll build her dreams and laugh and cry.
My lap is bare. I'm reconciled.
That girl is gone . . . she's yesterday's child.

Out of tune . . . weren't there days when you longed to be somewhere else, leading a different life? Why do all mothers make so many sacrifices?

Sacrifice

Sacrifice: To give up something for someone else.

Webster does not include the word "mother" in his definition of the word, but mothers seem to have a monopoly on it. They understand the essence of giving up some cherished moment or precious thing for their children. It wasn't until I became an adult with children of my own that I truly understood just how much my mother gave up to be my mother. The list is endless. I only wish that I had known enough to say thank you. Now, I say it silently every time I make a sacrifice for my children.

Out of Tune

I hum a song, a different tune . . .

But maybe some day far or soon,

I'll sing with those who fill my life,

And be in tune as mother and wife.

But until that day, I'll heed that song

That's filled my life, though right or wrong.

And as I grow to be more wise,

Perhaps I'll learn to harmonize.

Faded Photographs

I came across the faded photos of your life tucked between the pages of a weathered old photo album. I studied the wistful faces of youth smiling at me from those tattered pages, and I wondered: What dreams and aspirations are hidden behind the smiling eyes of the young girl who would grow up to be my mother, what secret longings reflected, what faded memories?

Now you sit beside me, sharing a cup of tea, your hair and face as faded as those old photos. I can still see the essence of the young girl reflected in those smiling eyes, the plans and dreams, and the faded memories of a life well-lived.

I love you . . . hello.

I never was one for saying goodbye when I left home, but I wasn't afraid to reach out because you had given me your love of life and the living . . .

Reach Out!

Reach out, my child, reach out and touch . . .
For the world is waiting to offer so much.
Gently touch as you're finding new friends,
And meeting the people your busy life sends.
Touch them with kindness to show that you care,
And listen with patience to the feelings they share.
Greet them with humor and smiles and your trust
As looking within becomes a real must.
Be ready, sweet one, to reach out and give,
And joy will be yours for the way that you live!

We were ready to take on the world, keeping in mind just who we were.

The Measure of My Life

God has given each of us a measure of life . . . our own set of standards, rules and goals. Some yardsticks are longer than mine, with different rules, inhibitions or restrictions.

They may be shorter, with more intuition and carefree feeling, taking one day at a time.

These tools for examining our lives belong to each of us alone. I cannot use your measure to guide my life, nor do you use mine. I must look to the given measure of my life, answering to no one but myself and my God.

And then we were gone, and you said . . .

You know that I can't ever bid you goodbye.
I won't ever say it. I won't even try.
Please carry my thoughts wherever you go.
I'll think of you, dear, and I'll love you . . .
Hello!

The essence of the man . . . this letter to you, dear Mama, would not be complete without mention of the man you loved so dearly, your husband, my father . . . for we are, you and I, what we are, far richer for having known and loved him.

The Essence of the Man

Picture his soul, the essence of man.
'Twas there the day his life began,
Sweet and pure from tiny seed,
Enriched with love, each kindly deed.
It grew each time he stopped to share,
To give someone a little care,
And let them known in some small way
That life's worth living every day.
He showed us all, the young and the old,
The way to heaven's sweet threshold,
Then slipped away and left our lives.
Yes . . . the man has gone, but his spirit survives.

Father and Son

For sixty years, they shared a name,

Those quiet men of gentle fame.

They walked together, as father and son,

Two lives enmeshed, their thoughts as one,

Toiling together through sickness and health,

Giving to all, dispensing wealth.

Their lives were a journey of endless sharing,

Quietly helping, always caring.

Yes, they gave their all to everyone,

The loving father, the laughing son.

So Quietly Loud

He gave all he had, whatever it took,

With only a gesture or one gentle look,

Touching our lives by the way that he lived,

Showing us all how to quietly give.

He was never unkind in word or in deed,

Always so willing to help one in need,

Cherishing days with his wife and his girls,

Polishing each like new shiny pearls.

That gentleman walked tall and proud.

He'd said it all . . . so quietly loud.

The Pain of Reminiscing

I spoke to you about my dad,

Of all the good times that were had,

By those of us who lived with him . . .

But memories overflow the brim.

So, I spoke to you about my dad,

Of how he smiled and made me glad

That I could say I was his girl . . .

Oh, what memories life unfurls!

Yes, I spoke to you about my dad.

You listened well, but I felt sad,

'Til I changed for bed and soothed my hurt,

By finally wearing his old shirt.

This Stranger Called Grief

Grief is no longer a stranger to me. Dad's gone now, his life snatched away abruptly. Lord, what a feeling, this thing called grief! How did I cope when my soul felt so empty, my heart so lonely, and oh, so very heavy? My throat ached with unvoiced cries, my eyes filled with unshed tears, not knowing what to do with the bewildering newness of this stranger called grief.

Today, my heart is no longer so heavy with grief. Yesterday, I shared it with my friend.

They'd been together for thirty-five years,
Through all the smiles and joyful tears.
Their love had grown day by day
And it showed in the things they'd do and say.
Their love endured the test of time,
And their life together was sweet and sublime!

Oh, for the days . . . how many times have we all felt that way, wanting to hold on to the memories of our youth? Those days are gone and yet the bond between mother and child still exists, as mysterious and precious as at the moment of birth.

Oh, For the Days

Oh, for the days when I came to your knee,
With sharing and caring and laughing so free.
Those days were so special and full of good things.
A treasure of love made us as rich as most kings.
No cares had I, nor tales of woe,
No secret sorrows you didn't know.
You shared my hopes, my moments, too,
When unborn dreams could not come true.
I couldn't begin in a thousand years,
With words or hugs or silent tears,
To tell you what they meant to me,
Those days, I sat there at your knee.

Those days may be gone, and we are apart,

But I'm oft at your knee . . .

Within my heart.

Daydreamers Two

Oh, that I could just be there,
To be with you, to laugh and share,
To fill my cup and bonds renew,
To quench my thirst for talks with you.

I shall be there to laugh and live.
Oh, yes, dear Mama, to care and give.
We'll share the day, the pot of tea . . .
And won't you build some dreams with me?

We do manage to get everybody together now and then on special occasions, and someone always seems to bring up some silly thing we did as kids and asks that proverbial question . . .

Remember When?

Thanksgiving's passed for one more year,
A day for warmth of food and cheer,
Of too much turkey, pies and such,
And lots of time to smile and touch.
We all sit back, so full and fed,
To reminisce and plan ahead.
Then Grandma's pictures pass around,
And "oohs" and "aahs" of joy abound.
There's time to play "Remember When?"
We're all the victim now and then,
Of stories shared from yesteryear,
With giggles, laughs and wistful tears.
Then dirty dishes beckon hands,
As feast and fun for all disbands.
We pack the kids, the food, the men . . .
Thanksgiving's blessed us once again.

You shared our triumphs and mourned our private losses as your own, small as they were, and somehow managed to save those precious days of our lives.

Mama's Trunk

Mama always had a large wooden trunk tucked away in the corner of her room. Daddy made it for her a long time ago with his large and loving hands, carving her initials just above the lock. As children, we were never allowed to look inside, and although it was not locked, we never did. It was always understood that it was Mama's trunk. We never knew what secrets were stored within, but what imagined belongings we often placed inside that weathered old box!

Since my family moved frequently, we were always leaving a part of ourselves behind, but Mama's trunk was always there, a silent, sturdy symbol of home. Sometimes, though, it was not just a trunk. It became a magic carpet for wide-eyed little girls at bedtime when Mama carried us away to faraway places and faces, and all through the pages of books. In the middle of wintery weather days and plays, it was an anchor for indoor tents, a stage for silly skits and songs, and a home for paper dolls. It was a painful stumbling block for stubbing toes in the dark when seeking solace from Mama after a dreadful dream. When my adolescent anguish brought me to my knees and into Mama's private place, it was there to lean on!

Years went by, and then one day, Mama opened her trunk to share its secret with us, and oh, what treasures lay within . . . from yellowed christening gowns and bronzed baby shoes to letters from a homesick college kid . . . all precious bits and pieces of our childhood lovingly tucked away all those years. Yes, Mama handed out her treasures, one by one, and they are dear to us now and always shall be.

Oh, yes, we shed a few tears that day, many in the shared joy of remembering the good times we had and knowing that we could share them with our own children someday . . . and all thanks to Mama's trunk. Oh, by the way, I, too, have a wooden trunk. Do you?

Treasures in a Trunk

What treasures hide within this trunk?

Is it full of wonders or a pile of junk?

Some mamas kept their precious things,

Even silly dime-store rings,

A christening gown, a baby's shoe,

Faded photos, just a few.

There may be letters from a homesick kid,

With news of all the things she did,

All bits and pieces of childhood years,

That remind us of laughs and tears.

Mothers and Daughters

Mothers and daughters, like the sand and the
sea,

Have a tenuous bond, connected, yet free.

The sea shapes and molds wherever it will,

Creating a need only it can fulfill.

It comes to its source and offers its treasures.

They rejoice in its triumphs and share all its
pleasures.

In the pools of the shore, these wonders unite,

And the delicate balance of nature feels right.

But the tide is always leaving the sands,

Turning its back on the shifting demands.

When the shoreline seems to grasp and hold,

It is often left with the wind and the cold.

The sea storms and rages as though with no care

For the wavering strength of the one who will
share

The interdependence, those delicate ties,

As long as there's life and the earth and the skies.

And after the tears of a storm are spent,

A peaceful calm seems heaven–sent.

For the tide returns to hug the shore.

They are together, united once more.

Yes, mothers and daughters are the sand and the

sea,

But which one is you and which one is me?

If you'll watch and listen to the ebb and flow,

I'm sure that soon you will come to know

That mothers and daughters, through life's windy

waves,

Often change places . . . one seeks, and one

saves.

My Mother's Hand

When I was just a wee little girl,
She held my hand and watched me twirl.
I wiggled and giggled with joyful glee.
She set me free, letting go of me.
She held my hand on the first day of school,
Knowing that I would follow the rules.
I learned my numbers . . . 1, 2, 3,
And she was always so proud of me!
As I grew to be a mother and wife,
She held my hand and guided my life,
Loving my children as Grandmas do,
And they love their Grandma through and through!
Now, I hold my mother's hand,
Hoping she knows and understands
The strength of the love she's given me,
As I let go and set her free.

When I think about my mother, many things come to mind, but one special thought stands out among all the rest. There is no one in all the world that I would rather call my mother.

Love,

Cherry

Epilogue

My mama is gone from this earth. I like to think that she and Daddy are having a second honeymoon in Heaven! I can't bring myself to write the last part of this book to describe what it is like to lose a mama. I keep thinking that I'm ready to try, but it just makes me cry.

Someday . . .

www.ingramcontent.com/pod-product-compliance
Lightning Source LLC
Chambersburg PA
CBHW040849120626
46547CB00001B/92